The Box

Written by Andrea Brooks
Illustrated by Linda Bird

Phonics Skills

Short a			Short e			Short i		
an	Pam	Cat	yes	let	bed	big	did	in
can	had	tan	red	fed		it	sit	
fan	flat	pan						
ham	bad							

Short o			Short u		
odd	box	Tom	jump	yum	fun
Fox	on	hot			
not					

"What an odd, big box!"
Pam Cat said.
"Can I see?"

"Yes, you can," said Tom Fox.
Tom Fox did let Pam Cat
see in the box.

Tom Fox had a tan bed
in the big box.
Tom Fox can jump on it.

Tom Fox had a red fan
in the big box.
Tom Fox can sit with the fan on.

Tom Fox had a flat pan
in the big box.
Tom Fox fed Pam Cat hot ham.

Pam Cat had hot ham
with Tom Fox.
Yum, yum! They had fun.

"Not bad for
an odd, big box,"
Pam Cat said.